AZERBAIJAN'S ECOSYSTEM FOR TECHNOLOGY STARTUPS
BAKU, GANJA, AND SHAMAKHI

Aimee Hampel-Milagrosa, Nariman Mannapbekov, Orkhan Babayev, and Sabina Jafarova

OCTOBER 2022

Country Report No. 5
Ecosystems for Technology Startups in Asia and the Pacific

ASIAN DEVELOPMENT BANK

Contents

Tables, Figure, and Boxes

Foreword

Technology-based startup enterprises—or tech startups—are an increasingly important part of the business landscape in Central Asia. These enterprises use new technologies to create new products or services or to provide services in a new way. Most startups will not survive, but some will succeed and make an important contribution to economic development. Tech companies like Facebook, Google, and Amazon are among the largest companies in the world today, and tech companies like Tencent, Gojek, Grab, Keepface, and Whelp are also among the leading emerging companies in Asia. The technology and dynamism they provide are important for economic growth.

Tech startups do not grow in a vacuum. They need access to funding, often from venture capitalists; skilled personnel, including experts in technology and business; good digital infrastructure; and supportive government policies. A strong ecosystem is critical for turning new ideas into commercially viable businesses. Given their growing importance, it is important to better understand the ecosystem in which tech startups develop.

This report assesses the state of tech startups in Azerbaijan with a focus on the startup ecosystem. It examines the extent to which the system supports the growing number of startups in the country. The report does not focus on any sector, although interviews with edtech and greentech founders were used as the main input for the analysis. Edtech and greentech were chosen because startups in these sectors not only become successful businesses but can also have a strong impact on development.

In this series of reports, tech startup hubs are almost always located in the capital city. An added value of this report is the inclusion of the cities of Ganja and Shamakhi in the analysis of the tech startup ecosystem—along with Baku. The report combines research and stakeholder interviews to provide a comprehensive overview of Azerbaijan's tech startup ecosystem. It provides recommendations on how the government and other stakeholders can strengthen the ecosystem to help tech startups thrive in Azerbaijan's major and secondary cities.

Albert Park
Chief Economist
Asian Development Bank

Acknowledgments

This report was prepared by Aimee Hampel-Milagrosa, Nariman Mannapbekov, Orkhan Babayev, and Sabina Jafarova. Aimee Hampel-Milagrosa, along with Paul Vandenberg and Matthias Helble, guided the research project. Rana Hasan and Lei Lei Song provided overall management support. The Azerbaijan Resident Mission of the Asian Development Bank (ADB) reviewed the report and solicited comments from the Government of Azerbaijan.

The authors would like to thank key experts from ministries, incubators, accelerators, development partners, investors, academic institutions, and startups who provided invaluable insights that were essential to the preparation of the study. The authors would also like to thank ADB Digital Technology for Development Unit (SDCC-DT) who supported the initial background report and Steinbeis and Ekvita Consultancy, who prepared the *Diagnostic Report on Fostering Development of Local Tech Startups in Azerbaijan for ADB*, which was also used in the preparation of this report.

The draft report was reviewed by the State Agency for Public Service and Social Innovations, the Ministry of Digital Development and Transportation, and the Ministry of Economy of the Republic of Azerbaijan, who provided extensive comments and suggestions. Their participation is greatly appreciated and has helped provide a more detailed review of the government's activities in the tech startup space in Azerbaijan, especially since the outbreak of the coronavirus disease (COVID-19) pandemic. Tuesday Soriano copyedited the report, Joe Mark Ganaban provided layout services, and Amanda Isabel Mamon provided administrative support, contracting, and manuscript management.

Abbreviations

ASAN	State Agency for Public Service and Social Innovations
ASAU	Azerbaijan State Agricultural University
ATU	Azerbaijan Technological University
CVC	corporate venture capital
GSU	Ganja State University
GDP	gross domestic product
ha	hectare
ICT	information and communication technology
MDDT	Ministry of Digital Development and Transport
MOT	Ministry of Transportation, Communication, and High Technology
R&D	research and development
SMBDA	Small and Medium Business Development Agency
SMEs	small and medium-sized enterprises
STEM	science, technology, engineering, and mathematics
VC	venture capital

Executive Summary

Azerbaijan is no newcomer in the international tech startup community. The Azerbaijan startup ecosystem took shape in the early 2010s with the country's first major startup event, Startup Azerbaijan, held in 2012. That same year, two of the country's largest telecommunication operators jointly launched Applab, an incubator for tech startups dedicated to developing new mobile apps. The Pirallahi High Tech Park, the country's first tech-oriented business park, was also established by decree that year. In Azerbaijan, mobile telephone operators were a key player in shaping the early ecosystem. This was partly because they had an interest in promoting new apps that they could buy up or that would increase usage of their services.

Despite slow growth, the government's full support for tech startups in Azerbaijan is undeniable. In 2016, the Strategic Roadmap for the Development of Telecommunications and Information Technologies identified information and communication technology as a priority sector to support economic diversification with digital innovation as a key objective. Following this high-level directive, the government mobilized the Ministry of Transportation, Communication and High Technology—renamed the Ministry of Digital Development and Transport (MDDT) in 2021—with the main mandate of supporting startups.

MDDT established the Innovation Agency, which remains the main branch of government responsible for organizing networking activities, hosting pitching competitions, collaborating with incubators and accelerators, courting venture capitalists, and managing high-tech parks. Currently, the Innovation Agency—which has been renamed Innovation and Digital Development Agency in 2021—can also issue startup passports, certificates that provide founders with financial and other types of government support. Several other government agencies are involved in innovation, such as the Agrarian Science and Innovation Center and the State Agency for Public Service and Social Innovations.

The Azerbaijani startup ecosystem has a large amount of capital, but not enough patient capital. Government funds have been allocated to startups, sometimes with funds originally intended for small and medium-sized enterprises (SMEs). The government is soliciting domestic and international private and corporate venture capital, and banks are encouraged to lend to startups. However, this has not led to a significant increase in risk capital for startups. Grants and prize money from competitions are not enough to help a startup scale up. Loans for SMEs can have unsustainable repayment terms for startups because they do not have the revenue to service the repayment while they develop their prototypes. Venture capital has not reached its potential because venture capital and tax laws are unclear.

The lack of sufficient capital and capital that is sufficiently patient for tech startups remains a key challenge for the ecosystem.

The number and commitment of Azerbaijani incubators and accelerators to foster the growth of tech startups is astounding. Most are headquartered in the capital, Baku, where a variety of incubators and accelerators operate, sometimes teaming up to offer specialized services. Some are highly specialized, while others have a broad goal. In the early 2010s, it was difficult to find and attract startups to incubation programs, but recently there has been a better balance between program demand and supply. Notable among incubators is their determination to include startups based in cities outside of Baku and in the surrounding area (Absheron Peninsula). Barama and Innoland, two of the most respected and prolific incubators in the country, have their programs further away, in cells in Ganja and Shamakhi, respectively.

Digital infrastructure and human capital are two areas where the government may need to focus more. There are large differences in the availability and quality of digital infrastructure between urban and rural areas. Digital infrastructure tends to be better and more accessible in Baku, while secondary cities with potential, such as Ganja and Shamakhi, are left out. In terms of human capital, historically low research and development spending, low enrollment rates in higher education, and low quality of teachers are problems that contribute to the skills gap. Baku-based universities are of higher quality and offer a more diverse range of courses than universities outside the capital. A look at the innovation efforts of Ganja State University, Azerbaijan State Agricultural University, and Azerbaijan Technological University shows the interest of educational institutions in promoting business startups. This interest needs to be further supported through investment in infrastructure, qualified teaching staff, and funding.

The results of this study lead to the following policy recommendations:

Facilitate government coordination in supporting tech startups. Coordination among the many agencies supporting Azerbaijan's tech startup ecosystem is necessary to eliminate overlap, make startup programs more efficient, and create synergies in the long term. From the startups' perspective, this will clarify responsibilities and make it easier to approach the appropriate agency.

Address legal and regulatory gaps. Addressing legal and regulatory gaps related to venture capital investment and taxation of innovative companies can reduce perceived risk for investors and founders. This could encourage more startups to form, lead to more venture capital flowing into Azerbaijan, and reduce the exodus of successful tech enterprises.

Invest in human capital. Skilled human capital is the foundation for a vibrant tech startup ecosystem. Continued investment in science, technology, engineering, and mathematics (STEM) education, not only in Baku but also in secondary cities such as Ganja and Shamakhi, is important.

Increase state support for the development of the tech startup ecosystem outside the capital. There is great potential for startups outside of Baku that remains untapped. Improving digital infrastructure and creating programs and policies that support the development of tech startups in secondary cities is a forward-looking way to ensure that no city is left behind.

Introduction

The 2015 oil price shock has encouraged Azerbaijan to reduce its macroeconomic vulnerabilities by diversifying sectorally beyond hydrocarbons. Economic expansion toward non-oil related manufacturing and services could ensure more stable and sustainable growth for the country. Therefore, along with the overall Roadmap for the National Economy and 11 other sectoral road maps, the Strategic Roadmap for Development of Telecommunications and Information Technologies was launched in 2016, identifying information and communication technology (ICT) as a priority sector to support economic diversification.

However, Azerbaijan's startup ecosystem began to take shape, albeit slowly, in the early 2010s. The country's first startup event, Startup Azerbaijan, took place in 2012. That same year, two of the largest mobile phone operators launched Applab, a tech startup incubator dedicated to developing new mobile apps. Pirallahi High Tech Park, the country's first tech-oriented industrial estate, was also established by decree that year.

In an era of falling oil prices in 2015 and the coronavirus disease (COVID-19) health crisis in 2020, digital technology has dramatically increased in the services it provides and the local companies it creates. Technology-based startups offer an opportunity to achieve Azerbaijan's economic diversification goals. Some of the world's largest companies are based on digital technologies: for example, Google, Facebook, and Amazon in the West, and Weibo, Grab, Gojek, Keepface, and Whelp in Asia.[1] These companies do not make tangible products but offer digital services, and many have expanded their reach as the global health crisis has worsened. Most of these companies began as small businesses with high scaling potential and have been appropriately labeled "startups" or "tech startups." For Azerbaijan to capitalize on this opportunity, not only do entrepreneurs need to take responsibility to develop and commercialize innovative ideas, but a supportive ecosystem is also needed to encourage, or at least not hinder, the development of startups.

---

[1]   Keepface is an Azerbaijani tech startup that provides an automated platform for influencers and advertiser interaction and content creation for internet marketing purposes. The company also manages marketing campaigns with real-time analytics.

This report examines the ecosystem for tech startups in Baku, with a special focus on the ecosystems of two secondary cities, Ganja and Shamakhi. As this report will show, much more can be done to diversify and expand the startup ecosystem in Baku and other cities by developing appropriate government policies, regulations, and programs.

This report also identifies the actors in Azerbaijan's startup ecosystem, their functions, and the gaps and weaknesses that may require attention and government support. The analysis is based on a review of the ecosystem, an examination of its components, and interviews with key stakeholders, including the startups themselves. The report focuses on improving the overall tech startup ecosystem, with the hope that it will also have important implications for the growth of startups in agritech (agriculture), cleantech or greentech (environment), healthtech (health), and edtech (education) to achieve the country's broader development goals.

Data and information for this report were obtained from multiple sources and in two phases. Face-to-face in-depth discussions were conducted in November 2019 with representatives from the Ministry of Digital Development and Transport, UNDP ClimateLaunchpad/Social Innovation Lab, Innoland, Bakcell Applab Center of Innovations, Youth Inc. as well as founders of two edtech startups in Baku and the founder of a greentech startup. A separate Asian Development Bank report, Fostering Development of Local Tech Startups, was completed in late 2021 and provided additional information used in the current report.[2]

---

[2] ADB. Fostering Development of Local Tech Startups Diagnostic Report (AZE TA-6650). Consultant's report. Unpublished.

Startups and the Startup Ecosystem

In a 2016 interview, Steve Blank, the father of startups analysis, defined a startup as "a temporary organization designed to look for a business model that is repeatable and scalable" (Kauffman Founders School 2016). The model is repeatable because it can be applied to different services and products. It is scalable because the business can grow rapidly. Scalability often comes from selling a service that can be replicated at almost no cost, such as an internet-based application (app) or a service delivered through digital access. The startup can quickly gain customers because the service is offered over the internet rather than in stores. Startups offer new products and services that provide innovative ways to solve problems with an approach that leverages technology.

Azerbaijan does not have an official definition of startups, but in 2021 it established the criteria for companies that can receive a tech startup certificate—also referred to as a tech startup passport (Table 1).[3] According to Decision No. 20 of the

Table 1: Eligibility Criteria for Tech Startup Certificate

	Criteria
1	The business is a micro or small business entity.
2	The founder is a resident taxpayer.
3	There is production of a product or service for the purpose of gaining income or profit.
4	The product or service is based on innovative initiative (for example, production or service processes in a new form, and there is application of new technology).
5	The product or service is competitive.
6	The business can forecast a reasonable increase in demand for their product or service in the short term (up to 3 years).
7	The product or service is not identical with any other in the market.

Source: ADB. Fostering Development of Local Tech Startups Diagnostic Report (AZE TA-6650). Consultant's report. Unpublished; and SMBDA. Startup Certificate.

---

[3] Article 13.2.80 of the Tax Code of the Republic of Azerbaijan provides the boundaries for startups definition. According to this article of the Tax Code, startups are entrepreneurial activities implemented on the basis of an innovative initiative, meeting the criteria set by the body Cabinet of Ministers of the Republic of Azerbaijan determined by the President of the Republic of Azerbaijan and carried out by the persons issued a "startup" certificate by the body State Small and Medium Business Development Agency supporting the development of micro-, small, and medium-sized entrepreneurship.

Cabinet of Ministers of the Republic of Azerbaijan dated 29 January 2021, holders of the certificate may access government services and programs for tech startups (Social Innovation Lab 2021). One of the main criteria is that the company must have an innovative product or service that is new to the market and is not intended for tech startups only.

The starting point of any startup is the prototype, which can become a minimum viable product. The prototype or alpha version is developed in the incubation stage. This is followed by acceleration and demonstration, where the prototype shows a faster development into a more concrete product. The product must be introduced to customers to gain users and thus revenue. While funding is important in all stages, for startups it is the initial and acceleration stage where a large volume of funding becomes relevant for scaling up. At some point, the team expands, and the complexity of the product may increase.

The ecosystem is the environment in which startups operate. There are five key components of Azerbaijan's tech startup ecosystem, as shown in the Figure: (i) government policy, (ii) finance, (iii) digital infrastructure, (iv) incubators and accelerators, and (v) human capital.

Other components of the ecosystem that may be important are suppliers, particularly those that produce hardware and physical products. Mentors are also important, although they are often associated with incubator and accelerator programs. Demand for the startup's product or service is critical to the startup's success. If a large portion of the potential market is made up of low-income households or people with limited technology or digital skills, demand for the new product or service may be low. Startups also need the basic conditions to do business, such as good energy and transportation infrastructure. Finally, a culture that encourages entrepreneurship and risk-taking—and does not stigmatize failure—can help bright individuals with good ideas to start businesses. Four other elements that are part of the startup ecosystem, but less prominent than those provided in the Figure, are suppliers, demand (customers), mentors, traditional infrastructure, and culture.

Figure: Tech Startup Ecosystem

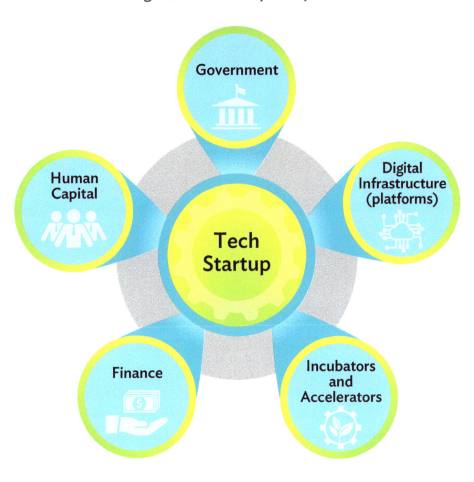

Source: Vandenberg, Hampel-Milagrosa, and Helble (2020).

Formation and Development of the Ecosystem

Innovation is the backbone of a digital-based economy. The Government of Azerbaijan is making efforts to improve the country's competitiveness, including its innovation ecosystem. According to the World Economic Forum's Global Competitiveness Report 2019, the evidence is mixed (Table 2). For example, while the business dynamism sub-indicator improved significantly from a rank of 73rd in 2015 to 23rd in 2019, the innovation sub-indicator improved from 61st in 2015 to 33rd in 2017 and slipped further to 68th in 2019.[4]

Table 2: The Global Competitiveness Index

Year/Indicator	2016 Ranking (among 140 countries)	2017 Ranking (among 137 countries)	2018 Ranking (among 140 countries)	2019 Ranking (among 141 countries)
Global Competitiveness Index pillars	40	35	69	58
Enabling environment				
Institutions	64	33	58	49
Infrastructure	65	51	46	38
ICT adoption	57	56	69	73
Macroeconomic stability	10	65	126	103
Human capital				
Health	102	74	91	98
Skills	89	68	54	48
Markets				
Product market efficiency	66	31	37	23
Labor market efficiency	30	17	40	21
Financial system	114	79	96	96
Market size	67	63	65	67
Innovation ecosystem				
Business dynamism	73	40	31	23
Innovation	61	33	71	68

ICT = information and communication technology.
Source: World Economic Forum. Global Competitiveness Index Reports. Geneva (various years).

---

[4] Azerbaijan was not included in the 2022 Global Competitiveness Index.

To innovate, a highly skilled workforce is needed. The skills sub-indicator in Azerbaijan improved dramatically from 89th in 2015 to 48th in 2019, thanks in part to education reforms introduced in response to the Strategic Roadmap for Vocational Education and Training introduced in 2015. The main objective of the education reforms was to increase the quality of education and strengthen the link between education and employment. The State Agency for Vocational Education was established in April 2016 under the Ministry of Education to align the vocational education system with the skills needed by the private sector and the labor market in general.

The country's overall position in the Global Competitiveness Index slipped from 2015. Azerbaijan ranked 40th out of 140 countries in 2015, 35th out of 137 countries in 2017, 69th out of 140 countries in 2018, and 58th out of 141 countries in 2019. ICT adoption also decreased from 57 in 2015 to 73 in 2019.

A deeper dive into the various subcomponents of the World Economic Forum's Global Competitiveness Report (Table 3) shows several indicators that point to the overall health of Azerbaijan's tech startup ecosystem. When the 141 countries are divided into thirds, with ranks 1–47 categorized as countries with thriving conditions for the assessed factor (green), 48–95 as midline (orange), and 96–141 as countries with poor conditions for the assessed factor (red), Azerbaijan's overall tech startup ecosystem is promising.

Table 3: Selected Subcomponents of the Global Competitiveness Report 2019

Index Component	Azerbaijan Score	Azerbaijan Rank from 141	Position
Internet users (as % of adult population)	79.8	43	
Digital skills among active population (1–7, best)	68.2	19	
Venture capital availability	52	24	
Entrepreneurial culture (0–100)	**62.1**	**22**	
Attitudes toward entrepreneurial risk	63.2	13	
Growth of innovative companies (1–7, best)	64.1	21	
Companies embracing disruptive ideas	56.6	18	
Research and development (0–100)	**19.8**	**111**	
R&D expenditures (%) GDP	6.2	94	
Innovation capability (0–100)	**38.3**	**68**	
International co-inventions (per million population)	1.2	96	
Patent applications (per million population)	4.6	83	

GDP = gross domestic product, R&D = research and development.
Source: World Economic Forum (2019).

The rating shows that there is a high level of digital literacy among the active population, and internet usage is also high. Venture capital is available, and the country not only has many innovative companies implementing disruptive ideas, but these companies also tend to grow. Azerbaijan's entrepreneurial culture is thriving. Azerbaijan has improved its position in a new Global Innovation Index 2021 rating of the World Intellectual Property Organization (WIPO). According to the report, Azerbaijan has improved its position by 2 steps compared with the 2020 rating and thereby ranking 80th among 132 states.[5]

However, the ranking in research and development (R&D) investment, which is somewhat correlated with the population's ability to innovate, could be improved.[6] The rate of co-inventions and patent applications could also be improved. Azerbaijan's Strategic Road Map for the National Economy Perspective, published in 2016, outlines a two-pronged approach to promoting human capital development by improving the quality of education at all levels and investing in R&D in areas that can increase labor productivity.

In the early 2010s, the number of Azerbaijani startups was small, and many were experimenting with ideas to develop innovative apps for phones and the internet. Applab had to search and find startups to join the incubator, and some that joined had little chance of success. In this way, the startup community grew with encouragement from above, but based on nascent entrepreneurial activity from below. Mobile telephone operators were a key player in shaping the system because they had an interest in promoting new apps that they could buy up or that would increase usage of their (phone) services.

Following Startup Azerbaijan, other events were held to promote the sector, showcase new startups, and connect with investors. Events include Mobile Mondays, university hackathons, pitching competitions, and presentations on startups.[7] The High Technology Park was built and equipped with coworking spaces that host mentors through their tech academy and provide networking opportunities. The High Technology Park held demonstration days to facilitate meetings with investors. The State Fund for Development of Information Technologies (ICT Fund) was established by the government to facilitate investment in startups. However, after several years of investment, not a single startup that had received a grant from the High Technology Park had developed an app or established a platform.

---

[5] Global Innovation Index 2021: Tracking Innovation through the COVID-19 Crisis.

[6] A brief discussion on Azerbaijan R&D investment is presented in section 4.5 on human capital.

[7] Mobile Mondays (MoMo) is an open community platform of key mobile phone industry players that fosters collaboration and B2B contact through live networking events.

A "startup carousel" began to emerge in Baku in which startups jumped from one program to another despite having limited success in the marketplace with their ideas. As a result, three government agencies—the Ministry of Digital Development and Transport (MDDT), the State Agency for Public Service and Social Innovations (ASAN), and the Small and Medium Business Development Agency (SMBDA)—initiated joint meetings in 2017 to discuss the right way to develop an enabling ecosystem for tech startups that would also stop the ongoing carousel. This paved the way for key tech startup players to begin sharing success stories and best practices with each other.

In 2016, the government identified ICT as a priority sector to support economic diversification. The Strategic Roadmap for Development of Telecommunications and Information Technologies was developed in 2016, with digital innovation as one of the main objectives. Two years later, the Innovation and Digital Development Agency and four companies (AzInTelecom, Lenovo, Nutanix, and iQRex) formed a consortium to improve access to financing for startups and encourage startups' participation in tenders for government projects.

Some startups have been successful. In 2021, Seedtable published a list of the top 33 Azerbaijani tech startups, including both high-growth scaleups and small creative startups, and almost everything in between.[8] Another 57 startups are featured on the Enterprise Azerbaijan platform's website for investors.[9] The startups' ideas are quite advanced, ranging from creating a laboratory for germinating synthetic gems (lab-grown former stones) to waste management solutions, each requiring an investment of up to $3 million. Azerbaijani startup Whelp (Caucasus Business Week 2021) is one of the 10 most successful startups in the world selected for the Techstars Toronto 2021 acceleration program. While these are isolated cases and say little about the overall performance of the startup development ecosystem, such success stories are important to point out. These successes can motivate potential founders to start businesses.

According to Startup Blink's startup ecosystem report, Azerbaijan has made efforts at the national level to promote the growth of tech startups and the innovation ecosystem.[10] For the ecosystem to grow, Baku should become a regional domestic hub and pave the way for seed funding in other cities such as Ganja and Shamakhi. The government recognizes the importance of digital development in transforming the economy into a knowledge-based economy and sees the growth of the ICT industry as a key component of the country's economic diversification away from hydrocarbons.

---

8   Seedtable. 33 Azerbaijan Starttups to Watch in 2021.
9   Enterprise Azerbaijan.
10   Startup Blink. The Global Startup Ranking.

The government now sees tech startups as a source of new ideas and productivity growth for the economy, as well as a driving force for the country's ICT sector and digital transformation. The success stories from Baku show that startups in the ICT sector can be successful and can be emulated in the country's secondary cities. On the one hand, this success is also a result of the government's previous and ongoing support. However, it is also forward-planning, because the current potential for founding innovative startups in the ICT sector is far from exhausted.

The ICT sector in Azerbaijan—which includes publishing, broadcasting, telecommunication, and computer information services—recorded revenues of AZN1.038 billion ($610 million) in 2017, equivalent to 1.5% of gross domestic product (GDP) and 2.2% of non-oil GDP in 2017. Of the total revenue, telecommunications accounted for 88%. In the same year, employment in the ICT sector amounted to 61,700 people, an increase of 11% compared with 2010 (ADB 2019). As part of the European Union's EU4Digital Initiative, Azerbaijan has taken on the role of a coordinating country for the "Innovation and Startup Ecosystems" component.[11] Among other support measures, the European Union promotes networking among innovation ecosystem actors. For the 2021–2027 funding period, the European Union announced programs to directly support startups, although these programs were not yet available as of February 2022. In line with efforts to develop the ICT sector, the Ministry of Economy established a new center for Industry 4.0 in 2021. The aim is to promote the development of the ICT sector and become a regional hub for Industry 4.0.

In February 2021 the President of the Republic of Azerbaijan approved the *Azerbaijan 2030 National Priorities for Socio-economic Development*. There are five national priorities identified: (i) sustainably growing competitive economy; (ii) society based on dynamic, inclusive, and social justice; (iii) competitive human capital and space for modern innovations; (iv) great return to the liberated territories; and (v) clean environment and "green growth" country. This once again underscored the central role that innovation plays in the country's development strategy.

Baku has become a vibrant center for startups because of the concentration of support on the Absheron Peninsula. There are two regional cities outside Absheron—Ganja and Shamakhi—that hold promise for tech startup development if the thriving ecosystem in Baku can be replicated.

---

[11]   EU4Digital. Azerbaijan.

Ganja is in the Ganja-Gazakh economic region with an area of 110 square kilometers. The city's population in 2021 was 338,000, which was more than a quarter of the region's population.[12] About 16% of Azerbaijan's agricultural production comes from this region, which indicates the important role of agriculture in this region. In terms of nominal monthly salaries, the region lags 1.5 times behind the national average. Ganja has an international airport. The most popular flight destinations are Istanbul (Türkiye), St. Petersburg and Moscow (Russian Federation), and Nakhchivan (Azerbaijan). People in Ganja are mainly employed in manufacturing, education, transportation, services, and the catering industry. Det-Al Aluminum is the largest employer in Ganja, followed by Ganja Auto Plant and Ganja Winery Plant.

Shamakhi is the most populous district in the mountainous economic region of Shirvan, but it is about 10 times smaller than Ganja. The population of Shamakhi city in 2021 was about 107,400, with most people employed in agriculture and related sectors. Shamakhi is less industrially developed than the city of Ganja, but economic conditions and living standards in Shamakhi have grown rapidly since the adoption of the State Program for Socio-Economic Development of the Regions of the Republic of Azerbaijan.[13] Most of the population of Shamakhi is engaged in animal husbandry and crop production, with emphasis on grains, potatoes, vegetables, melons, grapes, and fruits. In the 1970s and 1980s, Shamakhi became one of Azerbaijan's largest wine-growing regions, but since then grain production has expanded significantly. There are three agro-parks in Shamakhi that offer potential for agritech startup development. These agro-parks are Pasha Holding, Azersun Holding LLC, and AgroFresh.

---

[12] The State Statistical Committee of the Republic of Azerbaijan (in Azeri).

[13] Samaxi Ensiklopediyasi (in Azeri).

Components of the Azerbaijan Tech Startup Ecosystem

4

A startup ecosystem is an interrelated ensemble of components that support startups. This section analyzes five key components of the ecosystem for Azerbaijan: government support, digital infrastructure, finance, incubators and accelerators, and human capital. While the information is generalized for the entire country, the reality is that these components are concentrated in Baku. As added value, the report provides information and analysis on the startup ecosystems in Ganja and Shamakhi, two potential startup hubs outside the Absheron Peninsula. The goal is to assess the readiness of Baku and these two other cities to foster innovative activities and support the development of tech startups.

It should be noted that the components of the ecosystem overlap, and some activities straddle two or more of the five components of the framework (Figure). This is especially the case for government programs, as the government supports activities in the other components (such as finance, human capital, and digital infrastructure).

4.1   Government

Government policy in the form of rules and incentives is critical to developing a thriving startup ecosystem. It is essential for creating an environment that develops a culture of openness to risk and failure, supports innovative investment and entrepreneurship, and provides a platform for creativity and teamwork. In Azerbaijan, the government has pledged its full support for developing an innovative society and creating an enabling environment for tech startups. The state has initiated high-level road maps and established several innovation centers, which are described in this section.

4.1.1 Azerbaijan Strategic Roadmap for the National Economy and Roadmap for the Development of Telecommunication and ICT

The Azerbaijan Strategic Roadmap for the National Economy and the 11 sector road maps published in 2016 outline Azerbaijan's transition to an innovative economic structure starting in 2025 based on an innovative, well-educated, and competitive workforce. The road map supports the government's intentions to diversify the economy away from hydrocarbons following the 2015 oil price shock (Hampel-Milagrosa et al. 2020). The road map affirms that in a period of innovation-driven economic growth, the investment attractiveness of innovative sectors should be supported. It sets out specific tasks, such as supporting access to information and communication systems, improving ICT skills, and investing in education and research facilities. It also aims to improve the physical and technological infrastructure that supports the development of human capital.

Under the overarching strategic road map are 11 priority sector road maps, one of which is the **Roadmap for the Development of Telecommunication and ICT** (2016).[14] In it, skills development is prioritized as follows:

(i) Modernizing technological education with the participation of businesses and increasing technological literacy

(ii) Increasing ICT knowledge and skills, using ICT in the education system, reforming digital education to provide better ICT knowledge and skills, organizing courses to develop skills, and assessing skills and knowledge

In support of this sector road map, the 2016–2020 State Program for the execution of the National Strategy for the Development of Telecommunications and ICT was developed. This is discussed in more detail below in the section on digital infrastructure.

According to sub-paragraph 3.0.66 of the Regulations of the Ministry of Digital Development and Transport, it is among the MDDT's commitments to carry out through its subordinate body, the promotion of innovative activities, assistance to local businesses in obtaining modern technologies and technological solutions, and organization of their transfer, as well as support of innovation-oriented scientific researches, financing of innovative projects (including startups). The Ministry of Transportation, Communication and High Technology (MOT) has created high technology parks as industrial parks and incubators. The State

---

[14] Center for Analysis of Economic Reforms and Communication Electronic Monitoring and Evaluation Portal (2016) and Strategic Roadmap for Development of Telecommunications and Information Technologies in Azerbaijan Republic (in Azeri).

Fund for Development of Information Technologies (ICT Fund), administered by MOT, is the main government fund for the development of the digital ecosystem and the commercialization of innovative technologies. In 2018, the State Fund for Development of Information Technologies was subordinated to the Innovation and Digital Development Agency.

The Center for Analysis and Coordination of the Fourth Industrial Revolution (4SIM) was established under the Ministry of Economy by the Decree of the President of the Republic of Azerbaijan No. 1245 dated 6 January 2021. The purpose of establishing 4SIM is to strengthen the position of the Republic of Azerbaijan in the Fourth Industrial Revolution, which dictates the trends in the global economy and changes the rules of competition, and to ensure its place among the leading countries in this area. 4SIM carries out cooperation and coordination of the Republic of Azerbaijan with international organizations operating in the area of the Fourth Industrial Revolution, as well as analysis and coordination of challenges, initiatives, strategies, and projects in the digital economy. 4SIM also hosts the affiliated center of the Fourth Industrial Revolution Network of the World Economic Forum (WEF) under the agreement signed between the Government of Azerbaijan and the WEF on 1 April 2021. A memorandum of understanding was signed between 4SIM and the Turkish company Bulutistan on 10 May 2022. The purpose of this memorandum of understanding is to promote development of the startup ecosystem in the field of the Fourth Industrial Revolution technologies, to assist in the development of private sector digitalization, and to facilitate dialogue between the two countries' private sector on the application and use of cloud services. Within the framework of the memorandum of understanding, free cloud services will be provided to support startups and scale up for a specified period of time.

4.1.2 Innovation and Digital Development Agency (formerly Innovation Agency)

The Innovation and Digital Development Agency, under the Ministry of Digital Development and Transport, was established by Presidential decree in 2018. The agency supports entrepreneurs using modern technologies and technological solutions; promotes innovative scientific research and its transfer; supports innovative projects, including startups; and provides grants, credits, and venture capital. In October 2021, the name of the responsible ministry was changed to the Ministry of Digital Development and Transport, and the Innovation Agency was merged with the newly established Innovation and Digital Development Agency.[15]

---

[15] Ministry of Digital Development and Transport and Transport of the Republic of Azerbaijan. Innovation and Digital Development Agency Public Legal Entity. Decree of the President of the Republic of Azerbaijan No. 1464 dated 11 October 2021 "On some measures to improve governance in the field of digitalization, innovation, high technology and communications in the Republic of Azerbaijan."

The Innovation and Digital Development Agency currently manages two technology parks in Azerbaijan: the Pirallahi High Tech Park in Baku and the Mingachevir High Tech Park, near Ganja outside Baku. These two parks and other technology parks are discussed in the Digital Infrastructure section.

The Innovation and Digital Development Agency operates in Baku, but also works closely with startups in Ganja. As one of the main partners of the I2B from Idea to Business project, the agency organized startup competitions in Ganja in 2018 and 2019.[16] In 2021, the agency received the authority to issue "startup passports" to innovative companies, a mandate previously held exclusively by the Small and Medium Business Development Agency (SMBDA) (Azertac 2021). The issuance of startup passports is carried out in accordance with the "Rules for maintaining a public register of innovative projects and issuing a startup passport" approved by the Decision of the Cabinet of Ministers of the Republic of Azerbaijan No. 21 dated 29 January 2021, and this document is issued by the Innovation and Digital Development Agency under the Ministry of Digital Development and Transportation of the Republic of Azerbaijan from the date of adoption of the stated regulations. The agency also received approval to advise the ministry on the provision of funding to startups. Thus, the agency now plays an important role in providing technical and financial assistance to startups. A brief discussion of the financial activities of the Innovation and Digital Development Agency is presented in the Finance section.

4.1.3 Small and Medium Business Development Agency

The SMBDA was officially established in late 2017.[17] Its organizational structure was approved the following year. The SMBDA supports businesses across the country, including startups. The SMBDA categorizes startup founders as innovative SME entrepreneurs. It is the main and first government agency to issue startup passports, which provide privileges and special government support mechanisms for startups. As of October 2021, 19 startups had been awarded startup passports by the SMBDA (Box 1) (SMBDA 2021a).

In addition, the SMBDA provides a range of services to small and medium-sized enterprises (SMEs) and startups. The agency also coordinates and regulates various services provided by government agencies to SMEs and startups. Business development support is provided by the SMBDA in six general categories (Table 4).

---

[16] Azərbaycan Respublikası Regional Inkisaf Ictimai Birliyi (2018) and Azərbaycan Respublikası Rəqəmsal Inkisaf Və Nəqliyyat Nazirliyi (2019).

[17] The SMBDA was established under Part 1 of the Decree of the President of the Republic of Azerbaijan No. 1771 dated 28 December 2017 "On further improvement of small and medium business management."

Box 1: Reflections on the Startup Certificate

Startups and individuals can apply for a startup certificate. The certificate is issued by the Small and Medium Business Development Agency (SMBDA). Startup certificate holders can benefit from a tax exemption on income from innovative activities. Sole proprietors are exempt from income tax for a period of 3 years from the date of obtaining the startup certificate. For a startup that is at an early stage of development, the certificate is also a helpful tool to attract investors, as the SMBDA can act as an intermediary between local entrepreneurs and investors, both foreign and international financial institutions. The procedure for obtaining the certificate is transparent and easy to follow. However, the number of certificates issued is still low. Reportedly, fewer than 20 certificates were issued in the first 6 months after the program's launch. The total increased to 42 as of July 2022.

Source: Authors' interview with the SMBDA representative, 6 November 2021; SMBDA. Startup Certificate.

Under sub-paragraphs 3.1.12, 3.1.13, 3.1.25, 3.1.41–3.1.43, 3.1.46–3.1.50, 3.2.8, 3.2.11, and 3.2.28 of the "Regulations of the State Small and Medium Business Development Agency of the Republic of Azerbaijan" approved by the Decree of the President of the Republic of Azerbaijan No. 148 dated 26 June 2018, the following are within the rights and commitments of the SMBDA:

1. To support the registration of startups and the patenting of their innovative ideas;
2. To promote the interaction of startups and micro, small, and medium businesses with higher education and research institutions, industrial and technology parks, technology business incubators and technology transfer centers, as well as to take part in the activities of business incubators, industrial and technology parks and training centers in the relevant field;
3. To coordinate relations between entrepreneurs and industrial parks, neighborhoods, agro-parks, clusters, special economic zones, model enterprises, technoparks, and innovation centers existing in the country, and to promote their registration as residents of industrial zones together with relevant government agencies;
4. To support the expansion of to financial resources (loans, investments, grants, venture capital, etc.) for startups and entrepreneurs;
5. To provide financial support for individuals and startups with new business ideas for the organization of primary business activities, as well as to organize project financing through foreign grants and develop various programs and competitions in this direction;
6. To coordinate projects of donor organizations and nongovernment organizations that support startups and entrepreneurs and implement joint initiatives;
7. To support the identification and development of innovative entrepreneurs, building their capacity to benefit from technological innovation and conduct scientific research by entrepreneurs through the realization of various programs;

8. To make appropriate proposals for the establishment of technoparks and innovation centers to support research and development-oriented activities in industry and for the implementation of these activities;

9. To take measures to increase the effectiveness of the interaction between education, science, and industry, for entrepreneurs to benefit from the innovation infrastructure of universities and public and private research institutions, and to strengthen industrial and university cooperation;

10. To promote business support activities in innovative projects and investors' investment by investors in innovative enterprises;

11. To submit proposals to develop the association of entrepreneurs specializing in innovation;

12. To select innovative and knowledge-based projects to be carried out by entrepreneurs through competitions, to ensure the acquisition of funds in the form of one-time grants from international organizations and foundations, as well as their own financial resources, to provide them with technical, organizational and financial support;

13. To take measures to expand the application of scientific research and innovation by entrepreneurs, produce competitive industrial products, and provide services based on innovative high technologies; and

14. To interact with other government agencies and institutions in the sector, including using the existing infrastructure and network for public services, social innovation, and support for entrepreneurs.

Table 4: Business Development Support of the Small and Medium Business Development Agency

Category	Specific Support
Finance	Providing discounted financing mechanisms Supporting bank collateral and guarantees Providing investment incentives
Licensing	Support in obtaining licenses and permissions
Networking	Developing business relationships and network entrepreneurs
Marketing	Promoting e-commerce for small and medium-sized enterprises
Legal	Protecting entrepreneurs' rights
Overall support	Providing support for export Providing support to industrial parks, industrial neighborhoods, and technology parks Providing support to business incubators Providing lifelong learning

Source: ADB. Fostering Development of Local Tech Startups Diagnostic Report (AZE TA-6650). Consultant's report. Unpublished.

The SMBDA's services are available to SMEs and startups through its representative office in Ganja. In October 2021, the SMBDA launched its video training platform KOBIM for startups and those who want to start a new business. The online platform offers 180 courses covering all aspects of starting and running a business (SMBDA 2021b).

The government's distinction between SMEs and tech startups tends to be blurred. Startups start small and therefore small and medium-sized to begin with, but startups are very different from traditional SMEs and require a range of support measures from the government and other stakeholders. In Azerbaijan, startups are registered in the same way as traditional SMEs, which can be a problem if they scale up later. Startups can register as sole proprietors or as a legal entity (i.e., a company). Registration takes a few business days and is handled by the State Agency for Public Services and Social Innovation. The SMBDA—and more recently the Innovation and Digital Development Agency—assists businesses with registration and helps with registration with the Ministry of Taxes. In addition, a startup company can register specifically as a startup. However, the registration process is confusing, mainly because of the overlap of relevant authorities. It can take up to 6 months to complete the process.

After business registration, the factors affecting the growth of SMEs and startups begin to diverge greatly. Startups require different support services than SMEs to grow. For example, startups need patient capital, human resources, accounting, and legal advice to safeguard their innovative solutions.

Startups usually do not generate much revenue (or profit) in the first few years of operation. Therefore, they need patient equity capital—not loans. For this reason, some of the financial support mechanisms for SMEs and startups (i.e., loan programs) may be misguided. Amendments to the tax code in early 2019 will allow startups to be exempt from income tax for innovation projects for 3 years after registration (Government of Azerbaijan 2018). This can be seen as a useful support for startups but is hardly used as initial profits are low or zero anyway. The SMBDA has developed procedures that allow startups to operate tax free. The Cabinet of Ministers is considering extending the tax exemption period from 3 years after business registration.

According to interviews, some Azerbaijan legislation on enterprises, subsume startups under the umbrella of SME and foreign direct investment (FDI) legislation. The distinction and separate treatment of startups and SMEs in the legislation is not clear and needs to be clarified in the future. While the SMBDA is responsible for registering and supporting the growth of SMEs and startups, the Innovation and Digital Development Agency is the close ally of founders in technology and innovation. Some startup founders expressed concerns about lack of coordination between different ministries and agencies and called for a framework organization. A single and clear framework could be useful, or multiple framework organizations could collaborate in coordinating relevant organizations. An interview with one founder highlights the concerns (Box 2).

Box 2: Who Takes Regulatory Precedence?

To support innovative small and medium-sized enterprises and startups, various government agencies have adopted their own policies and programs. As a result, there is some confusion among startups as to which government agency takes precedence in terms of regulations. In addition, each agency has a different procedure for receiving support and different eligibility criteria.

Source: Authors' interview with a startup founder in Baku, 2019.

4.1.4 Agrarian Science and Innovation Center

The labor force of Azerbaijan is still heavily engaged in agriculture, and there is a need to improve agricultural productivity and move to high value-added agricultural production through modernization and agribusinesses. The goal of the Agrarian Science and Innovation Center is to develop agriculture on a more scientific basis by providing scientific and innovative support and advice to farmers. The center works closely with Azerbaijan State Agricultural University in the city of Ganja to promote innovative solutions, including support for digital startups.

In 2019, the Agrarian Science and Innovation Center organized the first AgroX Innovation Competition, a startup competition in partnership with the Ministry of Agriculture, Startup Azerbaijan, and Innoland (Nəbiyev 2021; Kerimkhanov 2019). The goal of AgroX is to support innovation in agriculture, promote agritech startups, and improve agricultural productivity through innovation and digital technology. A total of 52 projects were submitted for the competition, of which 12 were selected for a pilot phase.

4.1.5 ASAN Innovation Center

The State Agency for Public Service and Social Innovations (ASAN xidmət in Azeri) is an e-government portal that provides nearly 500 electronic services, including filing tax returns, registering businesses, and issuing licenses for businesses. The portal was established in 2012 and is an example of best practices in digitizing public services. One of ASAN's subordinate organizations is the ASAN Innovation Center. The center provides technical assistance to improve the use of information technology, systems, and resources in industry, finance, science, education, and other areas of the private and public sectors.[18]

---

[18]   See Innovations Center.

ASAN Innovation Center is one of the most active players in Azerbaijan's innovation ecosystem. In 2020, it organized 12 events, provided 360 hours of training, and supported 83 startups. In February 2020, the center established the Azerbaijan Innovation House in Silicon Valley, United States. In 2021, the center organized six incubation and four acceleration programs in Azerbaijan. It also aims to implement five projects in the education sector in the short term. The center is headquartered in Baku, but also works with startups in Ganja. In collaboration with the Agrarian Science and Innovation Center, the ASAN Innovation Center organized the AgroX startup competition in 2019 with 52 participating startups (Nəbiyev 2021). Since its establishment in 2012, the government has opened 15 ASAN centers nationwide. Some of these centers may be able to provide the kind of support offered by Baku-based incubators and accelerators.

4.2 Finance

Startups are constantly looking for venture capital, usually in the form of equity financing. Equity financing does not require servicing or regular repayment (like a bank loan), which is appropriate for startups because they have limited revenue or profits in the early years. Many startups require "patient capital," which is equity financing for new ideas with potential but no demand or expectation of immediate returns. The ecosystem may have a large amount of capital, but that does not automatically translate into venture capital for startups. The lack of patient capital for Azerbaijani tech startups remains one of the key challenges in developing the ecosystem.

4.2.1 State Fund for Development of Information Technologies (ICT Fund)

The Azerbaijan government established the State Fund for Development of Information Technologies (ICT Fund).[19] The ICT Fund together with the Azerbaijan National Academy of Sciences allocated between $70 million and $80 million annually to support tech startups (Yudin 2021). The fund supports innovation by

(i) providing concessional loans to startups through authorized banks;
(ii) providing equity and venture capital to startups to develop new technologies, software, and equipment and to commercialize innovations; and
(iii) awarding grants for the development of software products, innovative infrastructure projects, and e-services.

---

[19] The State Fund for Development of Information Technologies was abolished in 2018.

In addition, under MDDT, the **Innovation and Digital Development Agency** promotes innovation in the ICT sector, including the commercialization of new digital ideas. The agency has established a joint consortium to promote access to funding for startups, through various funding sources.[20] The agency has established partnerships with the United Nations Conference on Trade and Development (UNCTAD), Israel's Hanaco Venture Capital, and Iran's National Innovation Fund (Mammadova 2019).[21]

4.2.2 Private Venture Capital and Corporate Venture Capital

Venture capital (VC) is available in Azerbaijan as private VC and domestic corporate venture capital (CVC). In addition, the government has entered numerous partnerships with international VC organizations to provide blended public and private VC to startups. However, data on the volume of VC transactions in Azerbaijan is not available.

500 Startups in Cooperation with ASAN (also known as 500 ASAN)

500 Startups is a venture capital firm headquartered in the United States with team members in more than 20 countries. It has invested in over 2,400 companies worldwide. A new program has been launched in collaboration with ASAN to build an innovative startup ecosystem and infrastructure in Azerbaijan. Startups in the early stage of development can benefit from educational programs and networking activities organized by 500 ASAN to access the global market and foreign investors. 500 ASAN started its operations in 2021.

Venture Capital

CVC is provided to startups by several large conglomerates, including the State Oil Company, British Petroleum, Coca-Cola, and three Azerbaijani telecom operators. CVC investments are not enough to grow the business, and these large companies usually seek to invest in startups whose products or services could provide solutions for their own businesses. Interviews with Azerbaijani startups indicate that they also receive various in-kind services (e.g., technical inputs, guidance, access to networks, and mentoring) from large local companies, which they use to develop and scale their ideas.

---

[20] The consortium partners include AzInTelecom LLC, Lenovo, Nutanix, and iQRex.
[21] The memorandum of understanding with UNCTAD (26 October 2019) among other topics frames Azerbaijani startups' access to the global market.

Apart from CVC, there is little domestic VC. Because CVC is generally provided in small amounts, the supply of VC in the country is generally inadequate. Significant VC from foreign sources is not available.

As of 2021, the existing laws of Azerbaijan do not provide for restrictions on foreign investment, but there is also no law that specifically refers to foreign VC.[22] The Law on Foreign Investments provides for the establishment of foreign-owned companies and joint ventures in the country. The Law on Investment Activity also defines different types of investments and investors and the protection they enjoy. However, neither law specifically mentions foreign VC. This gap in the law discourages VCs from abroad.

As a result, startups that need VC can register and set up shop in countries where VC is available. For example, four promising Azerbaijani startups (Buglance, Keepface, PeakVisa, and Cryptoyote) have moved to Dubai. The more flexible VC environment in Dubai meant that larger investment amounts (over $500,000 per investment) are available. According to an interview with an Innoland representative, other reasons tech startups are moving to Dubai are as follows:

- Better digital infrastructure and digital connectivity;
- Better chances of selling a product globally because of access to stronger platforms;
- A larger market means broader demand for a startup's product; and
- Better laws governing revenue sharing ratio (between investor and founder).

In short, many startups can get early-stage funding from the government or public entities. Often, this funding comes in the form of loans and grants. While there appears to be enough support of this type, the total volume may not be sufficient for rapid scale-up.

4.2.3 Funding for Small and Medium-Sized Enterprises and Startups

Some funding programs for SMEs and startups overlap. Both SMEs and startups can access these programs if they meet the eligibility criteria. Most of these programs are new and have only existed since the late 2010s.

The **Mortgage and Credit Guarantee Fund** was established in 2005 to help SMEs and startups access bank loans by guaranteeing mortgage loans by entrepreneurs from authorized banks. While its main duty is to implement mortgage—as well

---

[22] UNCTAD Investment Policy Hub. Azerbaijan: Law on the Protection of Foreign Investments. Law No. 57.

as preferential mortgage lending—it also provides consulting services on debt management, risk assessment, and risk management for entrepreneurs.[23]

The Ministry of the Economy established the **Entrepreneurship Development Fund** in 2018 to support businesses in general. Part of the fund focuses on the development of innovative technologies used in non-oil sectors. The fund offers loans at concessional rates. Short-term loans of 3 years or less start at AZN5,000 (nearly $3,000). Larger loans of up to 10 years start at AZN1 million ($580,000) and are a maximum of 10 times that amount (ABC.az 2018).

The SMBDA operates a fund for education, science research, and support projects in accordance with the "rules for financing education, science, research and support projects related to development of micro, small and medium enterprises" approved by the Decision of the Cabinet of Ministers of the Republic of Azerbaijan No. 364 on 30 September 2020. The program is open to micro, small, and medium-sized businesses and individuals engaged in entrepreneurial activities without legal entity. Funding is up to AZN20,000 for a project of 3 to 12 months. This program is not specifically designed to support startups, but the eligibility criteria do not exclude them.

The Azerbaijan Youth Foundation Credit Program supports innovative startup ideas of Azerbaijani youth by offering loans at low interest rates (Box 3).[24] Startups can borrow up to AZN50,000 from partner banks and credit organizations with the foundation's support. However, the program was not launched because banks were unwilling to lend to startups due to the high risk involved. A changeover of the program from loans to grants is currently under consideration.

Box 3: The Azerbaijan Youth Foundation—Getting Started with Tech Startup Funding

It will be necessary to discuss with banks and convince them that startup ideas are promising, realistic, and profitable. This requires better prepared startups and can be achieved if startups receive more support in developing their business. Such support for startups would be important. However, one of the issues raised is why distributing funding for startups should (also) be done through the Azerbaijan Youth Foundation when there are already enough funding tools for startups. Instead, there should be a discussion about how the government can guarantee loans for startups—or how it can further use its own funds as loans for startups.

Source: ADB. Fostering Development of Local Tech Startups Diagnostic Report (AZE TA-6650). Consultant's report. Unpublished.

---

[23] Baku Stock Exchange. Mortgage and Credit Guarantee Fund of the Republic of Azerbaijan.
[24] Azerbaijan Youth Foundation.

4.3 Digital Infrastructure

Digital infrastructure plays a key role in a startup ecosystem, as many innovative companies need connectivity and a platform to offer their services. Since 2016, the Strategic Roadmap for the Development of Telecommunications and ICT has stimulated the development of digital infrastructure to support innovative companies. This is also supported by the country's focus on improving physical infrastructure such as roads, water, and electricity to diversify the economy. A diagnostic assessment of the country's overall infrastructure investment needs in transport, power, telecommunications, and water supply and sanitation shows that a sustained investment of 6%–7% of GDP is required over the medium term (Hampel-Milagrosa et al. 2020). While state-owned enterprises and the private sector are expected to contribute, most investments may have to be funded from the state budget.

The state program for 2016–2020 has been developed for the implementation of the National Strategy for the Development of the Information Society under the guidance of the Ministry of Digital Development and Transport (UNIDIR 2021). The envisaged action areas are directly related to innovation and ICT development, such as developing ICT infrastructure, expanding the country's transit information corridor potential to provide high-speed internet connectivity, strengthening scientific and technological potential, and expanding scientific research.

The Ministry of Digital Development and Transportation (MDDT) emphasizes the importance of cybersecurity for the development of a knowledge-based society. Table 5 lists the priorities of MDDT.

Table 5: Priorities of the Ministry of Digital Development and Transportation

Priority Areas
1 Development of Azerbaijan ICT infrastructure and services
2 Development of the high-tech sector
3 Strengthening of the scientific and technical potential for the development of high technologies
4 Development of "electronic government"
5 Establishment of ICT as a factor of the development of society
6 Provision of information security
7 Creation of technology parks and VC funds

ICT = information and communication technology, VC = venture capital.
Source: ADB. Fostering Development of Local Tech Startups Diagnostic Report (AZE TA-6650). Consultant's report. Unpublished.

Under sub-paragraphs 3.1.10, 3.1.18, 3.1.22, 3.1.31, and 3.1.36 of the "Regulations of the Innovation Agency under the Ministry of Transport, Communications and High Technologies of the Republic of Azerbaijan" approved by the Decree of the President of the Republic of Azerbaijan No. 545 on 22 February 2019, the following has been included in the MDDT's commitments: (i) to provide tech startups with access to international scientific publications in the relevant field, (ii) to sign agreements and memoranda of understanding (MOUs) on cooperation in order to create necessary infrastructure and favorable conditions for individuals and startups who have started innovative activities without establishing a legal entity under higher and other educational institutions, state, nongovernment organizations, and private organizations; (iii) to ensure implementation of the actions provided for in these agreements and MOUs and allocation of funds; (iv) to take measures to protect and acquire intellectual property rights for innovative projects (including startups), innovative products, and services; (v) to support the patenting of innovative ideas and state registration of intellectual property rights; (vi) to finance innovative projects (including startups) through grants, soft loans, and investments in authorized capital (including venture financing); and (vii) to form state orders for innovative solutions to issues arising from the country's Sustainable Development Goals and involve local executors, including startups in their implementation through by holding competitions.

The government has developed two high-technology parks, the ICT Park in the Pirallahi Islands and the Mingachevir Park. The Pirallahi Park supports the modernization of the ICT sector by conducting research and creating modern research centers for the development of new information technologies. Mingachevir Park specializes in computers and other electronic devices.[25] The parks offer tax incentives for the companies located there, including startup projects that receive grants from the ICT Fund.

In addition, there are three agro parks in Shamakhi owned by corporations that promote innovation in agriculture and carry out activities in cooperation with the Ministry of Agriculture. While these are owned by private companies, they provide opportunities for the public (such as farmers, students, universities, smaller companies) to participate in research and development of cutting-edge agricultural practices.

- The agro park of Pasha Holding Limited Liability Company was built on 42,000 hectares (ha) of which 15 ha are in the Shamakhi region. A grain warehouse with a capacity of 11,500 tons was built, a pivot irrigation system was installed on 7,000 ha, 94 pieces of equipment were purchased, and 23,330 ha were purchased. In September 2020, the agro park held training sessions for farm owners on agrotourism.

---

[25] International Association of Science Parks and Areas of innovation. Innovation Agency – Pirallahi High Tech Park.

- Azersun Shamakhi Agropark of Azersun Holding Limited Liability Company was established on 4,348 ha, of which 2,723 ha are in Shamakhi. A pivot irrigation system was installed on 2,600 ha, a drip irrigation system on 100 ha, 130 pieces of equipment were purchased, and a 2,000-head livestock complex was built. The park organizes learning activities for farmers, such as the automation of processes in the livestock buildings and the operation of a special electronic system to monitor the health and nutrition of the animals and the quality of the milk.

- Agro Fresh's Agro Park was built on 1,495 ha. It is in its initial phase, and it is planned to install a pivot irrigation system for 500 ha.

4.4 Incubators and Accelerators

There are several incubators and accelerators in Azerbaijan. Some are highly specialized, while others have a broader objective. In the early 2010s, it was difficult to find and attract startups to incubation programs, but recently there has been a better balance between demand and supply of programs. An important function of incubators is to create interactive channels between innovative entrepreneurs. Providing coworking spaces, mentoring, hosting hackathons, demo days, and pitching competitions are some of the most effective ways Azerbaijani incubators and accelerators encourage founders to interact in the ecosystem. The most tailored incubation and acceleration programs offer a holistic approach to supporting founders, from skills to mentoring, access to infrastructure, and networking.

4.4.1 Barama Innovation and Entrepreneurship Center

Barama Innovation and Entrepreneurship Center (Barama Center), the first business incubator in Azerbaijan, was established in 2009.[26] The Barama Center offers a 6-month support program that includes access to office space, professional consulting, training, and networking opportunities. It is managed by the government's Innovation and Digital Development Agency. The Barama Center reports that 45 startups have been founded in its 10 years of operation through 2017.

Outside Baku is the One Barama Center in Ganja, operated by Azerbaijan Technological University. Both the Barama Center in Baku and the One Barama Center in Ganja offer the following services:

- 3-month intensive program for business and product development
- 6-month support to launch a product

---

[26] Barama Innovation and Entrepreneurship Center is not in operation as of July 2022.

- Mentorship
- Support in networking with key ecosystem players
- Provision of coworking space
- A startup school

The Barama centers can serve as a template for other incubation and acceleration centers in Azerbaijan. For example, the NEXT STEP Innovation Center follows the Barama Center model and was established in collaboration with Innoland.[27]

4.4.2 Bakcell Applab Incubation Center

Another early incubator is the Bakcell Applab Incubation Center, known as Applab.[28] It supports digital software developers engaged in mobile app development and related technologies, from concept to launch. First, it had to find startups that wanted to join its activities. To do this, it used social media, presentations to university students, and other tools to seek out entrepreneurs. They were offered office space and access to cell phones, computers, laptops, and other equipment as models and for experimentation. They received further support in the form of mentors, participation in exhibitions, investors outreach, and specialized consulting.

Initially, 10 startups participated in Applab, but with limited success. The startups either had experienced developers with raw ideas or great ideas but no developers. The goal of Applab was to bring people and ideas together, but in the early days of the ecosystem's development, many startups were not used to sharing information. After a few more months of searching universities, colleges, and coworking spaces, more proto-startups were identified and joined.

4.4.3 Innoland

Innoland is one of the heavyweights in tech startup incubation in Azerbaijan, with a thriving office in Baku and an upcoming office in Shamakhi. Innoland has established itself as the country's main institution for business incubation and acceleration. Innoland Baku offers incubation, acceleration, and training programs.[29] The incubator offers a 6- to 12-month program for early-stage companies.[30] The 3-month accelerator program helps startups reach international markets and includes networking with at least 30 international mentors.[31]

---

27   See NEXT STEP (in Azeri).
28   Applab is not in operation as of July 2022.
29   Innoland representative interviewed by authors in Baku 18–20 November 2019.
30   Being a part of INNOLAND, the incubator is managed by NEXT STEP Incubation Center.
31   Being part of INNOLAND, the accelerator is managed by SUP.VC.

There is also a 12-week program that covers all aspects necessary for growth, including courses, mentoring, demo day, and participation in international startup events. Innoland Baku also offers a coworking space and virtual residence.

The eligibility criteria for joining the incubator are as follows: founders must be at least one person with a technical background and one with a business background; they must be between 25 and 30 years old and have at least 5 years of professional experience; and they must develop startups that are designed to be international from the beginning.[32] Innoland's startup portfolio for 2021 shows 17 startups housed in the Baku office. However, in 2021, Innoland stopped accepting applications for its incubation program due to COVID-19 restrictions.

Innoland Shamakhi will operate under the guidance of the Shamakhi Regional ASAN Service Center, located in the ASAN Hayat Complex. A final service offering for startups or potential founders has not yet been released by Innoland Shamakhi (as of early 2022). In general, the ASAN Service Center is open to Azerbaijani citizens from all regions of the country.

A joint incubation program was conducted by Innoland and Bakcell Telecommunications (Innoland 2018). Startups that qualify for Innoland's incubation program with Bakcell receive technical support in areas such as mobile app development, e-commerce, blockchain, gaming, 3D printing, and virtual reality and augmented reality. Selected startup teams receive mentoring from Bakcell and Innoland, access to Bakcell's network and media channels, and free office space. The incubation program goes beyond the usual business plan development support by providing (i) assistance in developing a proof-of-concept, and (ii) help in producing a minimum viable product.

Startup events are organized by incubator and accelerator programs, as well as other private and public actors. Events take different forms, but most allow startups to showcase their innovations and connect with investors, business leaders, international organizations, and government officials. Events include Startup Days (see Box 4), along with AgroX, Innofest, Idea to Business, Robopark, CyberWeek, Innovation Week, Baku e-Trade Forum, StartupFest, MainTech, Bakutel, Falcons Summit, AzCloud Hackathon, and Yeni Fikir. Many of these events are organized annually. In 2017, Bakcell, together with Telefonica O2 and its accelerator Wayra (from the United Kingdom), gathered the best 21 software startups from Azerbaijan to compete for a free spot in Wayra's 9-month accelerator program. Four companies reached the final round, but due to strong competition from other countries, none could win the top prize.

---

[32] See more information at Innoland and Startup Azerbaijan.

Box 4: Azerbaijan Startup Days

The 2-day Startup Days project, launched in 2019, promotes innovation in Azerbaijan, highlights new ideas of the youth, and creates a favorable environment for startups. Startup Days is aimed at strengthening internet business, innovation, startup movement, and organizing educational work, as well as promoting the formation of and networking among founders. On the first day, students will have the opportunity to meet with owners of local startups, well-known experts, and heads of local information technology companies. Students will have the opportunity to receive training in pitching and developing projects and prototypes. On the second day, there will be a pitching competition for the students' ideas and projects. With the help of mentors and experts, students develop initial versions of their projects. Selected business ideas will receive further support from Innoland.

Sources: Asan Xidmət (2019) and Shirinov (2018).

4.4.4 Other Notable Incubators and Accelerators

Technovate is a boutique venture program with the goal of creating at least one Azerbaijani startup worth more than $100 million by 2023. It was founded by Azerbaijani entrepreneur Farid Ismayilzada, who lives in California. Its venture studio model provides training and mentorship for early-stage startups and provides consultants and mentors to support the startup team (Anderson 2020). Technovate plans to expand globally in 2022.[33] **Sup.az** operates an accelerator for startups that offers a 3-month program for access to capital, mentoring, marketing, and product development. It is in Innoland. **Social Innovation Lab** helps emerging entrepreneurs develop solutions with global impact.[34] Its startup portfolio includes CO2 Catalyser, an electrochemical carbon dioxide converter; Sh2ower, a device that prevents water and energy loss; BioBone, an eco-friendly fertilizer; and PlastoFuel, a converter for plastic waste into liquid fuel. It collaborates with other incubators and accelerators, as well as with Baku Engineering University.

ClimateLaunchpad[35] supports entrepreneurs in the cleantech and greentech sectors. Its startup portfolio includes Airflec, an energy-saving solution for cars; Climasel, an energy-saving solution for homes and offices; and Eco Solutions, which provides waste collection solutions for hotels. **Youth Inc.**[36] manages business support programs offered by the Ministry of Youth and Sports, Coca-Cola, and Debate in Civil Society Public Union. It was launched in 2013 and its programs are open to startups.

---

[33] Technovate. About Us.
[34] Interviewed in Baku on 18–20 November 2019.
[35] Interviewed in Baku on 18–20 November 2019.
[36] Interviewed in Baku on 18–20 November 2019.

Some other organizations that provide incubation and acceleration services for startups are Innova Startup Factory, Qazan IMIC, Simbioz, and ADA Innovation Center. Many other ecosystem players have emerged in Azerbaijan which were not included in the report. These are Sabah Lab Acceleration Center, Khazar Ventures, Baku Investors Club, and Next Step Innovation Center.

The proliferation of incubators and accelerators for tech startups is one of the strengths of Azerbaijan's startup ecosystem. Startups are innovative and full of talent but may lack experience in running a business. Incubators and accelerators play a key role in providing the necessary support services that startups need to successfully navigate the tech and business world.

4.5   Human Capital

Human capital plays a crucial role in an innovative economy and in innovative companies such as startups. Interviews with Azerbaijani startups indicate that the country lacks people with technical expertise in science, technology, engineering, and mathematics (STEM) and people with multidisciplinary skills (STEM and business). It is necessary to have highly skilled specialists in various fields, but it is equally important to have people with multidisciplinary skills. Skills needed in the country include entrepreneurial skills, the ability to acquire patents, talk to investors, negotiate and speak in public, and the ability to formulate the terms of an investment. Creativity, vision, confidence, and motivation are soft talent components that are weak among local startups, according to an interview with an Innoland representative. When a few specialists get together, other talented people will want to join. Azerbaijan has human capital, but it is not enough to drive an innovative economy.

The development concept "Azerbaijan 2020: Look into the Future," a policy document published in 2012 on the website of the President of the Government of Azerbaijan, identifies innovation, research, and development as some of the most important issues that require development (Government of Azerbaijan 2012; Government of Azerbaijan—Presidential Website 2012). It states that knowledge-based, innovative, and science-intensive technological expansion is a priority to ensure sustainable development. The document also states the need to modernize infrastructure for science and ensure the digitalization of information support systems. It emphasizes the need to stop the "brain drain" caused by the exodus of bright minds and to create an innovative economy by strengthening the relationship between science and production.

However, R&D spending has not increased since the document was adopted in 2012.[37] R&D spending as a percentage of GDP peaked in 1998 at 0.42% and has since declined. According to the World Bank's World Development Indicators, it was 0.18% of GDP in 2018. In 2019, government expenditure on education was at 2.7% of GDP.[38]

Hampel-Milagrosa et al. (2020) cited the low number of higher-education enrollment and the low quality of teachers as two problems affecting human capital development in Azerbaijan. The country has the lowest enrollment rate in tertiary education in the region. Only about 30% of general education graduates enroll in university. This is most likely due to the centralized state quota system, in which "every year the government arbitrarily sets student admission quotas for all programs, whether government subsidized or self-financed, and in both public and private universities" (Aliyev 2011). In addition, teachers are generally underpaid and, as a result, schools are unable to attract and retain high-quality teachers. To address this problem, the Ministry of Education has organized a diagnostic evaluation of teachers since 2015. The salaries of those who successfully pass the diagnostic evaluation are increased.

In Baku, four universities offer courses on the development and teaching of information technology. These are Baku Engineering University, Khazar University, ADA University, and Azerbaijan Polytechnic University. Innoland established the Tech Academy, a coding school specializing in Python programming to prepare developers to work for startups that are in the incubation phase.[39] The academy had trained 72 apprentices as of January 2020. With Absheron-based universities already established, universities outside the capital may need to be more carefully considered for their potential contribution to the Azerbaijani tech startup ecosystem. The following discussion will focus on universities outside of Baku.

4.5.1 Ganja State University

Ganja State University (GSU) is a public university in Ganja. Officially accredited by the Ministry of Education, GSU is a medium-sized coeducational higher education institution.[40] There are eight faculties and more than 6,000 students.

GSU established a Department of Innovation in 2017. It has several subdepartments such as the ICT Office; the International Relations Office; the Office of Development of Information Resources; the Office of Strategic

---

[37] World Bank. Research and Development Expenditure (% of GDP)—Azerbaijan.

[38] See World Bank. R&D Expenditure (% of GDP); and Trading Economics. Azerbaijan – Public Spending on Education Total (% of GDP).

[39] Python is one of the most widely used programming and coding languages.

[40] Ganja State University.

Analysis, Evaluation and Monitoring; and finally, the Technology Transfer Office, which is directly responsible for issues such as business incubation, technology transfer, intellectual property protection, startups, and related projects. The Innovation Department provides the following services:

- Introductory training on innovation and entrepreneurship;
- Assistance in organizing events such as startup weeks and competitions;
- Mentoring on innovation and entrepreneurship;
- Assistance in preparing students for national competitions; and
- Assistance to students in finding grant-providing competitions.

GSU conducts its own startup competitions. In 2021, there were 62 student participants in 33 teams. Another 43 university employees participated in a separate competition category. The process for participating in the startup competitions is as follows: (i) business ideas are submitted; (ii) ideas with potential for success are selected; (iii) startups receive business development training; (iv) business ideas are presented at a pitch event at GSU; and (v) winners are sent to national startup competitions.

4.5.2 Azerbaijan State Agricultural University

Azerbaijan State Agricultural University (ASAU) is another public university in Ganja.[41] ASAU has more than 6,000 students and 560 academic staff. It offers 98 degree programs at graduate and undergraduate levels. The ASAU Innovation Center, which was established in 2018, provides support for startups. Support services are targeted to ASAU students and include (i) targeted training for students on a topic deemed necessary for a startup, and (ii) mentoring to prepare for participation in competitions and events.

The Innovation Center at ASAU offers incubation services to students who are already starting a business. The Innovation Center's business incubation service consists of four stages:

(i)   Idea discussion and assessment
(ii) Stage – Formation of startup team
(iii) Stage – Training
(iv) Stage – Creation of a product

ASAU has too few ICT teachers to create a large, skilled human capital base, and support is needed to increase teacher qualifications in computer programming.

---

[41] Azerbaijan State Agricultural University.

4.5.3 Azerbaijan Technological University

Azerbaijan Technological University (ATU) trains mechanical and technological engineers primarily in textiles, light manufacturing, and the food industry.[42] It is in Ganja and was founded in 1981. Administrative responsibility for startup development lies with ATU's International Department. A coordinator oversees the development of startups. Three lecturers support startups on a voluntary basis. Thus, there is no specific unit or department at ATU that formally provides services to startups.

ATU hosts the Ganja branch of the One Barama Center.[43] The results of the collaboration are still limited, and the number of active startups at ATU is small.

In summary, the human capital component of the startup ecosystem in Azerbaijan is critical, as tech startups require highly skilled talent. Investment in human capital plays an important role in increasing labor productivity, innovation, and competitiveness of goods and services. To reap the benefits of innovation, the focus should be on improving the quality of education in all higher educational institutions in the country—whether in Baku, Ganja, or Shamakhi. Continuous development of knowledge and skills in line with the evolving needs of the labor market is important.

The challenge for Azerbaijan is not only to improve the quality of general education, but also to build a higher education system that can foster and develop more highly technical skills (science and technology, engineering, and mathematics). To match education provision with labor market requirements, it is necessary to know what types of skill deficits—noncognitive, cognitive, or technical—exist.

4.6 Tech Startups

As in other countries, most startups in Azerbaijan are founded by a team consisting of at least one entrepreneur (a business-minded person) and one technology expert. In addition, the interviews suggest that Azerbaijanis who have successfully founded a startup tend to exhibit the following characteristics: they are passionate about what they do, willing to take risks, agile, with fluid responsibilities, take feedback seriously, and work almost around the clock to develop the product.

According to the interviews with Innoland Baku representatives and tech startup founders, there are three types of startups. First, there are those that were founded in the country and continue to work there. They have a high failure rate, which could be partly due to a lack of investment funds. Second, there are startups that

---

[42] See Azerbaijan Technical University.
[43] See Barama Ganja.

begin in the country but move to other countries to secure funding and growth opportunities. And third, there are startups by Azerbaijanis that are started abroad and remain abroad. These foreign-initiated startups are often located in the United Arab Emirates, as well as Estonia and Ukraine.

The most popular sectors for startups in Azerbaijan are e-commerce, mobile apps, fintech, edtravel, and edtech.[44] The most popular startups are Next Sale, Keepface, Buglance, Lia (Spinal), Sumaks, Bon.az, and AlKredit. Kvotter, which is also very popular, is described below, along with two other companies from the greentech and healthtech sectors.[45]

Edtech startup Kvotter is a social network and education startup that allows its users to scan and share quotes from books and other literary sources. Users can capture quotes with their phone's camera and share them on Kvotter or through other social media. The founders have developed an optimal character recognition scanner that converts text from an image into editable text. In addition, the reader can add hashtags and comments to the book quote. The app gives users access to millions of books because of its links to Amazon and other online booksellers. The founder began development, graphics, and web design in 2016. The startup was founded with the support of the Applab program. The company entered and won local competitions before officially launching in September 2016. The following year, the company won the internationally renowned Seedstars pitch competition in Switzerland.

Vriendly is a combined edtech and greentech startup serving as a virtual university for startups and entrepreneurs. Users can obtain personalized education and build their network by allowing virtual reality access to Silicon Valley personalities and resources—without having to physically travel. It allows users to interact "in-person" with other users. For example, a startup could use a virtual reality interface to connect with other startups, angel investors, and accelerators on the other side of the world. Students can engage with professors, mentors, and students at other universities in other countries via virtual reality. All parties can interact in real time. Vriendly provides entrepreneurs and students with peer-to-peer education with specified content. The company started to develop products in April 2018. Within 45 days, the founders developed 3D voice, peer-to-peer interaction, and other program features, enabling them to acquire their first customers and achieve business-to-business sales. After discussions and sales deals (in cryptocurrency) with Edumedia, the Ministry of Education, Barattson, Interpolymech Russia, and DMZ Accelerator Canada, the company developed its products further. The company plans to close its beta phase[46] and go public in 2021.

---

[44] Startup Blink.

[45] These were interviewed during the mission.

[46] Beta is a pre-release of software that is given out to a large group of users to try under real conditions.

Recommendations

Earlier sections of this report confirm broad government support for the creation and growth of tech startups in Azerbaijan. Based on the Strategic Roadmap for the National Economy and the Roadmap for the Development of Telecommunication and ICT, the government has established and mobilized several agencies tasked with supporting innovative companies. However, there are still areas where government support could be improved or expanded. This section focuses on key aspects of the startup ecosystem that could be improved. The recommendations are meant to be constructive and should be taken in that light. The following is a guide of what could be prioritized.

1. **Facilitate government coordination.** The analysis showed that the Government of Azerbaijan has mandated many agencies to support and fund startups. However, their proliferation could have an unintended negative effect—it confuses founders as to which agency is responsible for which function. Decision-making becomes complicated when it is unclear who takes precedence when functions overlap. A coordination or framework mechanism among these agencies is needed. The government could designate a coordinating body to promote interaction, cooperation, and collaboration among all public ministries, agencies, and centers working with startups. This body could organize regular meetings that promote information sharing among public agencies and provide startups with up-to-date information. It could also serve as a liaison for all private entities working with startups.

2. **Address legal and regulatory gaps.** There are legal and regulatory gaps in the startup ecosystem. While it is beyond the scope of this study to address the regulatory framework in depth, interviews revealed that the most cited gaps are the lack of a law on venture capital (VC) for innovative companies and suboptimal tax procedures for startups. Under current legislation, officially recognized startups are exempted from paying taxes for the first 3 years after company registration. However, since these first years are dedicated to the development of a minimum viable product—the startup does not generate profits—the legislation is not very useful.

These loopholes could encourage an exodus of promising tech startups. The government can learn from the experience of other countries in regulating VC, particularly from Asian tech leaders, such as Singapore, the United Arab Emirates (UAE), the People's Republic of China, and India. The UAE may be a good model, as four Azerbaijani tech startups have moved to the UAE because of a better legal environment for raising VC funds. Another option is to use a regulatory sandbox approach for policy changes that the government is unsure whether to implement. The government could create a sandbox to test the potential impact of a regulation on a small and defined scale. It could then make revisions before implementing the regulation on a larger scale. A regulatory sandbox for VC could be timely.

3. **Invest in human capital.** Since the launch of Azerbaijan's Strategic Road Map for the National Economy Perspective and the 11 sector road maps in 2016, the government has achieved initial success in improving the human capital stock for Azerbaijan. This is because human capital development is one of the four core objectives of the strategic road maps. The strategic road maps outline investments in all pillars of education to support human capital formation and development. However, since one of the 11 strategic road maps focuses on vocational education and training, there is an emphasis on technical and vocational education and training. The focus could be to improve the technical capacity of the active workforce by strengthening entry-level science, technology, engineering, and mathematics (STEM) in basic, technical, and higher education. STEM should be supported not only in Baku but also in other cities and towns in the country.

4. **Strengthen support outside the capital.** Analysis has shown that incubators, accelerators, and other support are concentrated in Baku—which is typical of many countries where tech startup hubs are emerging. This concentration makes it difficult for nascent startups to access support services and exacerbates the socioeconomic divide between the Absheron Peninsula and the rest of the country. It is important to increase human capital outside of Baku, implement programs, and establish facilities that could cater to potential startups outside the capital. Digital infrastructure outside of Baku can also be improved in terms of the allocation of resources for overall infrastructure investments.

References

ABC.az. 2018. Interest Rate on Subsidized Loans for Entrepreneurs in Azerbaijan to Be Cut to 5%. Baku.

Anderson, M. 2020. Local Startup Developing Wearable Posture Device Raises $450,000. *Sacramento Business Journal*.

Asan Xidmət. 2019. The Project Startup Days Has Been Launched. Baku.

Asian Development Bank (ADB). 2019. *Country Diagnostics: Azerbaijan: Country Digital Development Overview*. Manila.

Azərbaycan Respublikasi Regional Inkisaf Ictimai Birliyi. 2018. Projects to Be Transformed from "Idea to Business" Have Been Selected in Ganja (in Azeri). Baku.

Azərbaycan Respublikasi Rəqəmsal Inkisaf Və Nəqliyyat Nazirliyi. 2019. The Best Innovative Projects of Ganja Have Been Identified within the "From Idea to Business" Project (in Azeri). Baku.

Azertac. 2021. The "Rules for Issuing a Startup Passport" Have Been Approved. Baku.

Caucasus Business Week. 2021. Azerbaijani Startup Whelp Selected Among 10 Most Successful Startups in the World for the Tech starts Toronto 2021 Acceleration Program.

Center for Analysis of Economic Reforms and Communication Electronic Monitoring and Evaluation Portal. 2016. Strategic Roadmap for Development of Telecommunications and Information Technologies in Azerbaijan Republic. Baku.

Government of Azerbaijan. 2012. Development Concept "Azerbaijan – 2020: Outlook for the Future". Baku.

Government of Azerbaijan – Presidential Website. 2012. Policy – Azerbaijan 2020: Look into the Future Concept of Development. Baku.

Government of Azerbaijan. 2018. Law On Amendments to the Tax Code of the Republic of Azerbaijan. 30 November.

Hampel-Milagrosa, A. et al., eds. 2020. *Azerbaijan Moving Toward More Diversified, Resilient, and Inclusive Development*. Manila: ADB.

Innoland. 2018. Bakcell Started Cooperation with "Innoland".

Kauffman Founders School. 2016. Startups.

Kerimkhanov, A. 2019. Government Applies Innovation Technologies in Agriculture. *AzerNews*.

Mammadova, L. 2019. Innovation Agency to Establish New Partnership with Hanaco Venture. *Azernews*.

Ministry of Digital Development and Transport of the Republic of Azerbaijan (MDDT). 2019. Consortium Established to Support Startups. News Release. Baku.

Nəbiyev, V. 2021. The Project of Ganja State University Was the First in the Startup Competition. Yeniavaz.

Shirinov, R. 2018. Startup Days to Be Held in Azerbaijan Soon. *Azernews*.

Small and Medium Business Development Agency of the Republic of Azerbaijan (SMBDA). 2021a. 19 Entrepreneurs Have Already Received the "Startup" Certificate (in Azeri).

SMBDA. 2021b. Entrepreneurs to Use Video Training Platform (in Azeri).

Social Innovation Lab. 2021. Criteria for Determining the Startup and the Rules for Issuing a "Startup Passport".

United Nations Institute for Disarmament Research (UNIDIR). 2021. Azerbaijan Cybersecurity Policy.

Vandenberg, P., A. Hampel-Milagrosa, and M. Helble. 2020. Financing of Tech Startups in Selected Asian Countries. *ADB Institute Working Paper Series*. No. 1115.

World Economic Forum. 2019. *The Global Competitiveness Report 2019*. Geneva, Switzerland.

Yudin, N. 2021. The Challenge of Raising Capital in Azerbaijan. Startup Universal.